Young Magician Card and Magic Tricks

Oliver Ho
Illustrated by
Dave Garbot

Main Street
A division of Sterling Publishing Co., Inc.
New York

Library of Congress Cataloging-in-Publication Data Available

2 4 6 8 10 9 7 5 3 1

Published by Sterling Publishing Co., Inc.
387 Park Avenue South, New York, NY 10016
© 2005 by Sterling Publishing Co., Inc.

This book is comprised of materials from the following Sterling Publishing Co., Inc. titles:
Young Magician Card Tricks © 2003 by Oliver Ho
Young Magician Magic Tricks © 2003 by Oliver Ho

Printed in China
All rights reserved

Sterling ISBN 1-4027-2920-0

For information about custom editions, special sales, premium and
corporate purchases, please contact Sterling Special Sales
Department at 800-805-5489 or specialsales@sterlingpub.com.

Contents

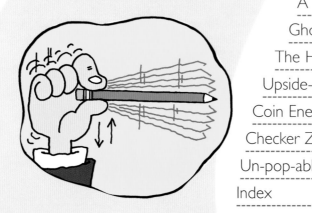

Card Lessons

All magicians know card tricks and if you want to become a magician, you'll need to learn a few. But before you start, you'll need some simple lessons about cards, like how to hold the cards, how to spread them, and how to cut and shuffle them. You will also need to know some "card words." These are the names of the different parts and marks on the cards.

Once you've gone through these card lessons, you can start learning the tricks. Make sure to ask an adult for help if any of the tricks are too hard. Always practice the tricks in front of a mirror so that you'll know how to do them perfectly. You can also try the tricks out in front of a friend who will promise to keep your magic secrets.

Important Card Words

Here are some words you'll need to know to do the tricks in this book.

Value: The value of a card can be a number (two to ten), an Ace (which equals one), or a court card (Jack, Queen, or King—a Jack equals eleven, a Queen equals twelve, and a King equals thirteen).

Suit: A card can be one of four suits: Clubs, Hearts, Diamonds, and Spades.

Face: The face of a card is the side that shows its value and suit.

Back: The back of a card is the side with the pattern on it. It's the side that doesn't show the value of the card.

Faceup: To have a card faceup is to show the face of the card.

Facedown: To have a card facedown is to show the back of the card.

Deck: A deck is what you have when all the cards are stacked one on top of the other.

Edges: When you look at a card or at the deck, there are four edges: the top edge, the bottom edge, the left edge, and the right edge. The top and bottom edges are also called the short edges. The left and right edges are also called the long edges.

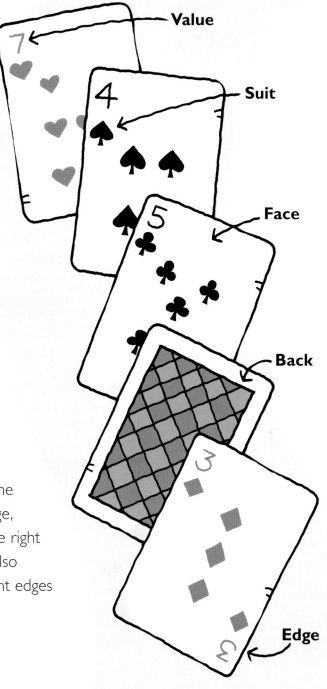

Value

Suit

Face

Back

Edge

Finding the Right Deck

When you do card tricks, you need a deck that fits in your hand. You should start with a child's size deck when you are learning the card tricks.

How to Hold the Deck

Hold the deck facedown in your left hand. Place your first finger around the short edge, like in this picture.

Now you're holding the deck like a real magician. This is called the magician's grip.

How to Square the Deck

To square up the cards, you just straighten up the deck so that all the edges are even.

Before Squaring...

After Squaring

How to Spread the Cards

When you ask someone to "pick a card," this is the best way to spread the cards out for him: Hold the deck in your left hand and push some of the cards over to your right hand, like in these pictures below.

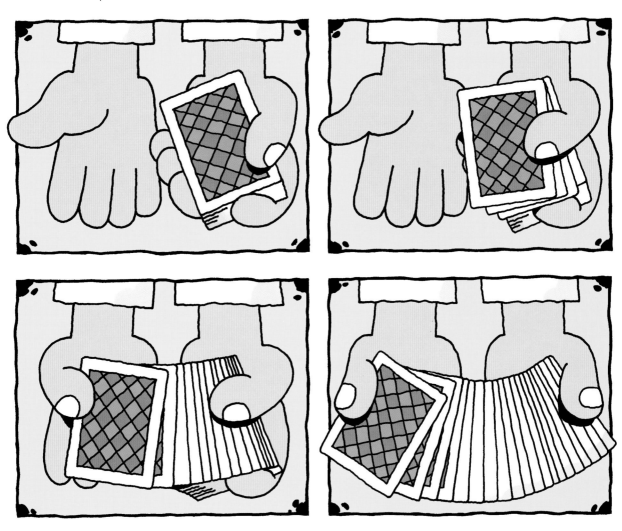

How to Cut the Cards

To cut the cards means you take the top half of the deck and move it to the bottom. You can do this in your hands or on the table.

To cut the deck in your hands, hold the deck in your left hand and follow the pictures.

To cut the deck on the table, place the deck on the table and follow the pictures below. Make sure you square up the deck after cutting the cards.

How to Shuffle

Shuffling the cards is an easy way to mix them all up without making a mess. One of the easiest ways is called the overhand shuffle.

1. Hold the deck in your left hand.

2. Take some cards from the bottom with your right hand.

3. Pull some cards from your right hand into your left a few times.

4. When all the cards are back in your left hand, square up the deck.

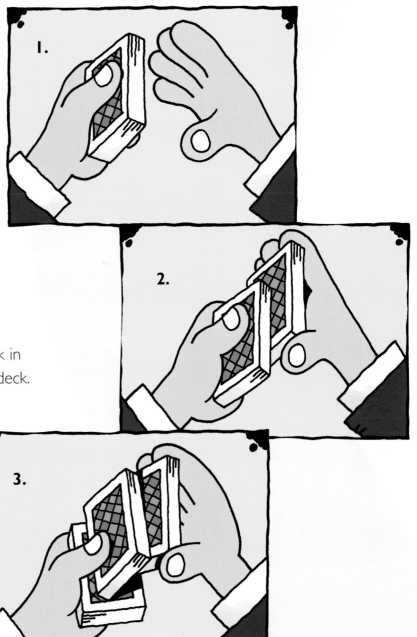

The Rising Card

The Magic

A card floats out of a deck you're holding!

The Trick

1. Hold the deck up in your right hand so that your audience can see the card on the bottom of the deck.

2. Tap the top edge of the deck with the first finger of your left hand. When your finger touches the deck, secretly stick out the little finger of your left hand and use it to push the top card partway up. Make sure to do this slowly. If you wiggle your little finger when you push the card up, the card will look even more like it's floating.

Amazing Aces

The Magic

After you put the two black Aces and the Ace of Diamonds in different parts of the deck, they show up together in the middle of the deck, and the Ace of Diamonds has been turned over.

Before You Start

Take all the Aces out of the deck. Then take the Ace of Diamonds and turn it over so that it's the only card that's faceup. Put it on the bottom of the deck.

The Trick

1. Hold the two black Aces in front of the Ace of Hearts. Spread the two black Aces apart so you can see just the tip of the heart behind them, like in the picture. This creates an optical illusion. The tip of the heart looks like the top part of the diamond.

2. Show the three cards like this to the audience. Tell them you have the Ace of Clubs, the Ace of Spades, and the Ace of Diamonds. Then square up the cards and put them facedown on top of the deck.

3. Take the top card, call it the Ace of Diamonds, but make sure that no one sees that it's really the Ace of Hearts. Stick the card into the middle of the deck.

4. Take the new top card, show it to the audience, and put it on the bottom of the deck. Make sure that no one sees the Ace of Diamonds, which is hidden and turned over on the bottom of the deck.

Black Ace

Ace of Diamonds is faceup on the bottom of the deck

5. Turn the top card over to show the audience, then put it back on top of the deck. Tell your audience that you put the Ace of Diamonds in the middle of the deck. Then you put one of the black Aces on the bottom of the deck and the last one is on top of the deck.

6. Cut the deck. You can cut it a few times, if you like. Make a magical pass over it and then spread the cards to show the Ace of Diamonds turned faceup in the middle of the deck.

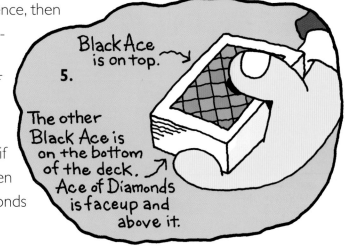

Black Ace is on top.

5.

The other Black Ace is on the bottom of the deck. Ace of Diamonds is faceup and above it.

6.

7. Take out the Ace of Diamonds and the two cards just below it. Turn them over to show the two black Aces.

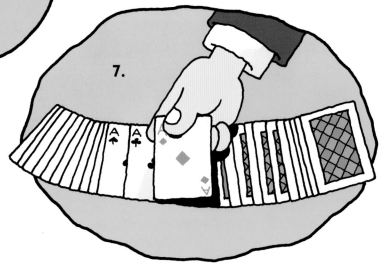

7.

The Perfect Prediction

The Magic

You put out three cards and ask someone in your audience to choose one. When she does, you show a piece of paper that says she would choose that card!

What You'll Need

Three slips of paper   *A pen*

Before You Start

Take any three cards from the deck. For example, let's say you use the Two of Clubs, the Ten of Diamonds, and the Queen of Hearts.

Set out the three slips of paper.

On one slip of paper write, "You will choose the Two of Clubs."

On the second piece of paper write, "You will choose the Ten of Diamonds."

On the third write, "You will choose the Queen of Hearts."

Now here's the real secret: Hide each of these pieces of paper in a different place. For example, you can put one of them in your left pocket, one in your right pocket, and one in your back pocket. Make sure you remember which pocket each note is in.

You can also hide the pieces of paper in much stranger places, such as in each of your shoes, under a chair that your audience is sitting on, or taped to the bottom of the table. Use your imagination to find three places to hide the papers, but be sure to remember where you hid each one.

Put your three cards on top of the deck. Make sure you know what order they are in.

The Trick

1. Deal out the top three cards so that they are facedown on the table. Ask someone from your audience to point to one of them.

2. As soon as she points to one, you know which card she's chosen. Tell her to wait before she turns it over. Take out the piece of paper with that card written on it.

3. Tell her that you knew which card she would choose.

4. Turn the piece of paper over at the same time she turns her card over. Show her that the card matches what you wrote on the paper.

The Key Card Method

The most popular card tricks are "pick a card" tricks. You ask someone to choose a card. You can't see what card she chose but you find it in some magical way.

One of the easiest ways to do these tricks is to use a secret that magicians call the "key card" method. Once you know this secret, there are a lot of different ways you can use it.

1. Spread out the cards and have someone from your audience take a card from the deck.

2. While she's looking at her card, turn around. Tell your audience you're turning around so you can't see her card. But what you're really doing is looking at the card on the bottom of the deck. Remember this card. It's your key card for this trick.

3. Turn back and ask your friend to put her card on top of the deck. You can also put the deck on the table and ask her to put her card on top of it.

4. Cut the deck (or ask her to do it). This will put your key card next to hers. You can cut the deck as many times as you want, but make sure you do not shuffle it. That would move the key card away from her card.

5. Look through the deck. When you see your key card, her card will be to the right of it.

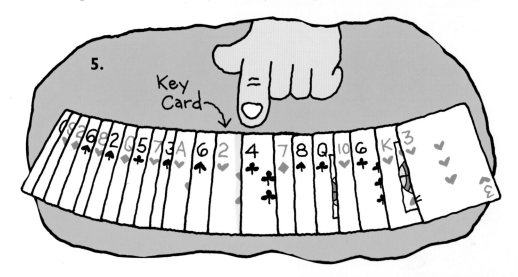

6. Take her card out from the deck and show it to her and the audience.

Now there are a lot more "magical" ways to show her card. We'll show you six different ways over the next few pages.

Fingerprints

The Magic

You find a card that someone from your audience chose by studying the cards for fingerprints.

The Trick

1. Following the key card method (see pages 18–19), ask someone from your audience to choose a card.

2. After you or your friend has cut the deck a few times, leave it on the table. Then ask to see your friend's hand. Tell him that you're studying his fingerprints.

3. Pick up the deck and hold it facedown. Deal the cards

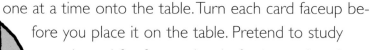

one at a time onto the table. Turn each card faceup before you place it on the table. Pretend to study each card for fingerprints before you place it on the table.

4. Once you get to your key card, the very next one you deal will be your friend's chosen card. When you turn his card faceup, pretend to study it, and tell him that you found his fingerprints.

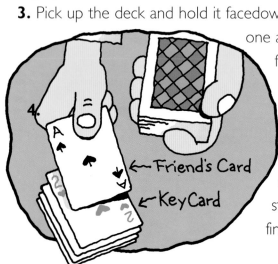

← Friend's Card

← Key Card

The Next Card

The Magic

Someone from your audience chooses a card and hides it in the deck. You deal the cards one at a time on the table. When you get to her card, you promise your friend that the next card you turn over will be hers. She thinks you're wrong, but you show the card and it's hers!

The Trick

1. Following the key card method (see pages 18–19), ask someone from your audience to choose a card. Then cut the deck a few times.

2. Hold the deck facedown. Deal out the cards one at a time. Turn each card faceup before placing it down on the table.

3. Once you see your key card, you know the next one will be your friend's chosen card.

4. Deal out your friend's card and pretend you don't know that it's hers. Deal out a few more cards on top of her chosen card.

5. Tell your friend that the next card you turn over will be hers. But because she has already seen her card, she will think you're wrong.

6. Instead of dealing the next card, look through the cards you've already turned over. Find the card that you know is your friend's. Turn it facedown and then turn it faceup. Just like you promised, the next card you turned over is hers!

Lifting Weights

The Magic

You find your friend's card by weighing it in your hand. It is more "magically" heavy than the other cards.

The Trick

1. Use the key card method to place your friend's chosen card next to the one that you know (see pages 18–19). Hold the deck facedown. Then start turning the cards faceup one at a time.

2. Pretend to weigh each card in your hand before you drop the card on the table. Tell your friend that he added magic to his card when he chose it. The magic makes his card weigh more, but only a magician can feel the added weight.

3. When you turn over your key card, you'll know that the very next card will be your friend's. Pretend that his card feels heavier. Tell him this must be his card.

KEY CARD:

Mind Reader

The Magic

You find your friend's card by reading her mind!

The Trick

1. Following the key card method (see pages 18–19), ask your friend to choose a card. Cut the deck and place it facedown on the table.

2. Tell your friend to think about what's on her card because you will try to read her mind.

3. Pretend to be thinking hard and then act as if you're starting to see something.

4. Turn the deck faceup on the table and spread the cards to the right. Look for your key card. When you find it, take out the card to the right of it. This will be your friend's card.

Key Card ⟶   ⟵ Friend's Card

Inside Out

The Magic

Someone from your audience chooses a card and it ends up being the only card that's face-up in the deck.

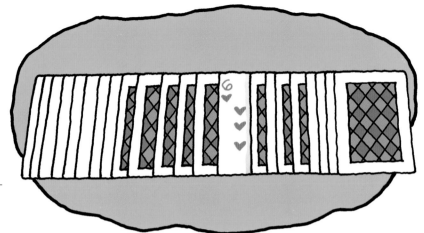

The Trick

1. Following the key card method (see pages 18–19), ask someone from your audience to choose a card. Cut the deck a few times.

2. Look through the deck. Tell your friend that you're trying to find his card.

3. When you find your key card, cut the deck so that the key card is on the bottom of the deck.

3.

Friend's Card on the top →

Key Card on the bottom

4. Your friend's card should be the top card on the deck. Square up the cards and tell your audience that you're having trouble finding your friend's card.

5. Hold the deck behind your back.

6. Tell the audience that you're going to try to find your friend's card without looking at the deck.

7. Take the top card (your friend's card) and turn it over. Stick it in the middle of the deck. Square up the cards.

8. Ask your friend to name his card. Then spread out the cards facedown on the table. His card will be the only one that's faceup.

Inside Out Again

The Magic

Here's another way to do the last trick:
Someone from your audience chooses
a card. That card magically turns
faceup in the deck.

Before You Start

Hold the deck facedown. Turn
the bottom card over so that
it is faceup. Now you're ready
to begin.

The Trick

1. Spread out the cards and ask someone in the audience to pick a card. Make sure no
one can see that the bottom card is faceup.

2. After your friend chooses a card, turn away from her and ask her to show the card to
everyone.

3. While you're turned away, secretly turn the deck over in your hand. The deck is now faceup but it looks facedown because your bottom card is on top.

4. Turn around. The audience will believe the entire deck is still facedown. Take your friend's facedown card. Without looking at it, stick her card into the deck.

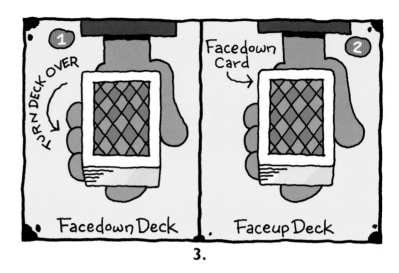

3.

5. Hold the deck behind your back and tell your audience that you'll try to find her card. What you're really doing is turning the bottom card faceup.

6. Spread the cards facedown on the table. Her card will be the only one in the deck that's faceup.

Turn bottom card faceup behind your back

5.

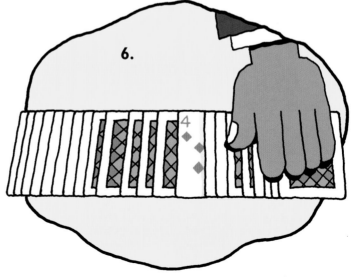

6.

The One-way Deck

The Magic

Someone in your audience picks a card from the deck. You turn around while she shows the audience her card. She puts the card back into the deck. You can tell which card she picked.

Get a One-way Deck

The secret to this trick is the type of deck you use. Look at the pictures on the back of different decks. Some decks have a pattern on the back that looks the same whether the cards are right-side up or upside down. Other decks

Right-side Up   Upside down

have pictures on the back so that you can tell when the pictures are right-side up or upside down. Magicians call these "one-way decks."

Before You Start

Turn all cards so the pictures on the back are right-side up.

The Trick

1. Spread the cards out for your friend to choose a card. After she picks her card, turn away with the rest of the deck in your hand. Tell her that you don't want to see the card.

2. What you're really doing is turning the deck around so that when she puts her card back into the deck, it will be the only one where the picture on the back is upside down.

2.

Turn Over Deck

3. Turn back to face her and ask her to put the card back into the deck. Make sure that her card will be the only one with the upside-down picture on its back. If it isn't, ask her to show everyone the card once more. Turn the deck around while she is doing this.

3.

4. Once her card is in the deck, you can shuffle and cut it as many times as you wish. Her card will be easy to find. You only need to look at the backs of the cards and pick out the one where the picture on the back is turned over.

5. As you did with the "key card tricks" (see pages 20–28), you can show your friend's card in a lot of different ways:

✦ You could just pull it from the deck.

✦ Cut the cards so hers is on top and deal it out to her.

✦ Cut the cards so hers is on the bottom. As you square up the cards, secretly look at her card. Cut the deck again so that she doesn't see her card. Then pretend to read her mind.

Use your imagination to come up with more ways to show her card.

The Four Thieves, Part 1

The Magic

While telling a story about four robbers, you show everyone the four Jacks and then place them into four different parts of the deck. When you give the top of the deck a magical touch, all four Jacks show up together there.

Before You Start

Take the four Jacks and three other cards out of the deck. Hold the four Jacks so that they face you.

Put the three other cards behind the last Jack. If you turn this packet of cards face-down, the three cards are on top and the four Jacks are below them.

Take a King out of the deck, and leave it faceup on the table.

4 Jacks are on the bottom.

The Trick

1. Hold the packet of seven cards. Leave the deck facedown on the table. Spread out the four Jacks so that everyone can see them.

2. Make sure that you don't show the three cards hidden behind the last Jack. Your audience should believe you're only holding four Jacks.

Three cards hiding behind last Jack.

2.

3. Tell your audience that you will be using these four Jacks to tell a story. They are four thieves who want to rob a building.

4. Square up the packet and place it facedown on top of the rest of the deck. Tilt your hand down a little so that your audience is looking at the back of the deck instead of the edge of it.

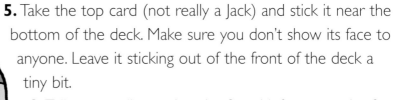

4.

5. Take the top card (not really a Jack) and stick it near the bottom of the deck. Make sure you don't show its face to anyone. Leave it sticking out of the front of the deck a tiny bit.

6. Tell your audience that the first thief went to the first floor.

7. Take the next card (not a Jack) from the top of the deck and stick it into the middle of the deck. Again, make sure not to show its face. Leave it sticking out a little bit.

8. Tell your audience that the second thief went to the second floor.

9. Take the next card from the top (not a Jack). Without showing its face, stick it close to the top of the deck. Leave it sticking out a little like the others.

10. Tell your audience that the third robber went to the third floor.

11. Turn over the top card and show everyone that it's a Jack. Turn it facedown and stick it into the deck about one or two cards from the top. Leave it sticking out like the others.

12. Tell your audience the fourth robber went to the fourth floor, which was near the roof.

13. Slowly square up the deck. Push in the four cards. Make sure no one can see the faces of the cards that are sticking out. Place the deck facedown on the table.

14. Tell your audience that just as the thieves were looking around, an alarm went off. Tap the top of the deck and make a sound like a ringing bell.

15. Take the King that you left on the table and tell your audience that this is a police officer. Put it facedown on top of the deck.

16. Deal out the top five cards. You should have the King followed by the four Jacks.

17. Tell your audience that the police officer chased all four thieves to the roof and caught them.

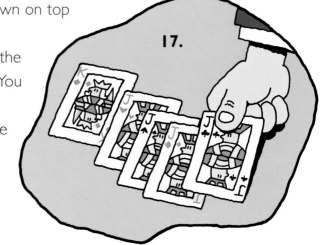

The Four Thieves, Part 2

The Magic

This is another way of doing the last trick. You put the four Jacks at different places in the deck. You cut the cards once and then all the Jacks come together.

This trick is a little easier to do than the last trick. You don't have to hide as many cards in your hand and you can show more of the Jacks to the audience during the trick.

Before You Start

Take out the four Jacks, two other cards, and a King. Leave the King faceup on the table. Hold the four Jacks. Place the two other cards behind the third Jack.

Two other cards hidden behind Jack number 3.

The Trick

1. Show the four Jacks to the audience. Make sure no one sees the two other cards hidden in them. Square up the cards and place them facedown on top of the rest of the deck.

2. Take the top card (a Jack) and show it to the audience. Then place it on the bottom of the deck. Tell them the first thief waited on the first floor.

3. Take the next card (not a Jack). Don't show this card to the audience. Stick it near the bottom of the deck. Tell your audience that the second thief went to the second floor.

4. Take the card (not a Jack). Again, don't show this card to the audience. Stick it near the middle of the deck. Tell your audience that the third thief went to the third floor.

5. Turn over the top card (a Jack). Tell your audience the last thief waited on the roof.

6. Place the King facedown on top of the deck. Tell your audience this King is a police officer and a magician. Cut the deck.

7. Turn the deck faceup and spread the cards. The King will be between the four Jacks.

8. Tell your audience that the magic police officer caught all four thieves.

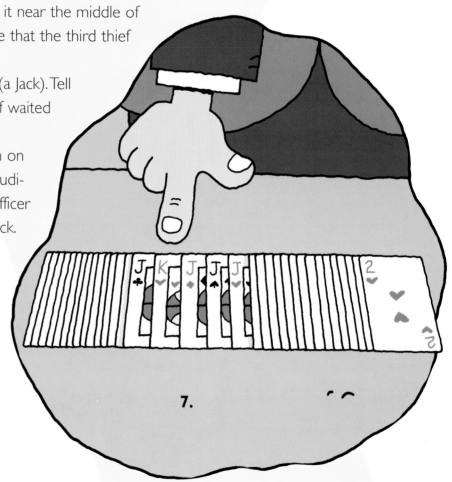

7.

Messy Shuffle

The Magic

You mix the deck so that some cards are faceup and others are facedown. By making one magic cut, you bring them all facing one way.

The Trick

1. Hold the deck facedown in your left hand. Take a small bunch of cards from the top into your right hand.

2. Turn the cards in your right hand faceup and put them on top of the cards in your left hand.

2.

3. Take all the faceup cards and a bunch of facedown cards into your right hand. Turn these over and place them back onto the deck. Keep doing this until you've gone through the entire deck.

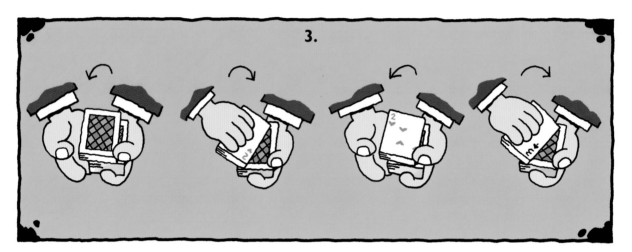

4. It looks as though the deck is completely mixed up with faceup and facedown cards. But the deck is really divided into two halves. Their backs are just facing each other.

5. Find the place where the two halves meet and separate them. Turn one half over and shuffle them together.

6. Now you can spread the cards to show that they're all facing one way!

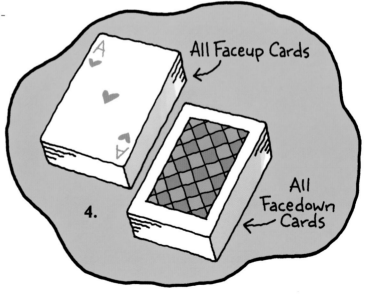

All Faceup Cards

All Facedown Cards

4.

Divided Deck, Part 1

The Magic

You cut the deck into two piles. Someone from your audience chooses a card from the first pile and places it into the second pile. You shuffle the second pile and then find his card right away.

Before You Start

You need to divide the deck into two groups. One group should have all the red cards (all the Hearts and Diamonds). The other group should have all the black cards (all the Clubs and Spades).

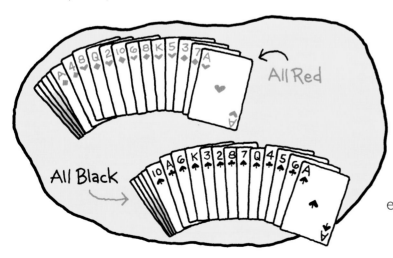

All Red

All Black

The Trick

1. Hold the deck so that it faces you. Divide the deck in half so that you have one deck that has all the red cards and another one that has all the black cards. Place each deck facedown on the table.

4.

Deck 2

2. Your audience should believe that you've just cut the deck. They don't know that you've divided the red and black cards.

3. Ask someone from your audience to point to one pile. Whichever pile he chooses, spread those cards from that pile so that they are facedown on the table. Ask him to pick a card. After he takes one, square up the pile that the card came from and put it away.

4. Ask him to show everyone the card. Then tell him to put the card facedown into the second pile of cards on the table.

5. Pick up the second pile of cards and shuffle it as many times as you wish. Turn the cards so they face you. Ask your audience to think of his card.

6. Look through the cards for the one card that is a different color from the others.

7. Take his card out and place it faceup on the table. Shuffle the two halves of the deck back together so no one will discover your secret.

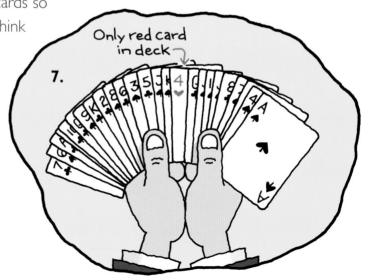

Only red card in deck

7.

Divided Deck, Part 2

The Magic

Here is another way to do the last trick: You divide the deck in half. Someone from your audience chooses a card from the first pile and places it into the second pile. After shuffling the second pile, you can find her card right away.

Before You Start

In the last trick, you divided the deck into reds and blacks. The only problem with that trick is that if your friend turns over any of the decks, she will know your secret. The way we do this trick is a little safer.

Instead of dividing the deck into reds and blacks, this time divide it into four suits (Hearts, Clubs, Diamonds, and Spades). Make sure one half of the deck has all the Hearts and Clubs. Make sure the other deck has all the Diamonds and Spades.

Hearts &
Clubs

Diamonds &
Spades

The Trick

1. Hold the deck so it that faces you. Divide the deck so that all the Hearts and Clubs are in one deck and the Diamonds and Spades are in another deck. Place each deck face-down on the table.

2. Ask someone from your audience to point to one pile. Whichever pile she chooses, spread those cards from that pile so that they are facedown on the table. Ask her to pick a card. After she takes one, square up the pile that the card came from and put it away.

3. Ask her to show everyone the card. Then tell her to put the card facedown into the second pile of cards on the table.

4. Pick up the second pile of cards and shuffle it as many times as you wish. Turn the cards so they face you. Ask your friend to think of her card.

5. Look through the cards for the one that has a different suit than the others. In the deck that has only Hearts and Clubs, look for the Diamond or Spade. In the deck that has only Diamonds and Spades, look for the Heart or Club. Take out that card and place it faceup on the table.

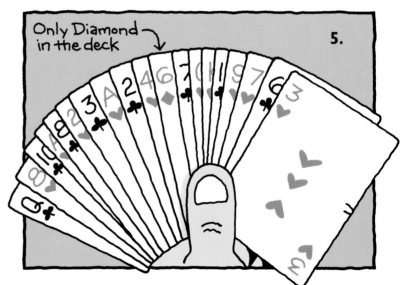

Only Diamond in the deck

5.

6. You can repeat this trick, if you like. If people accidentally look through the cards, they probably won't notice that the two piles are divided into suits.

Two-card Prediction

The Magic

You pull out two cards from the deck and place them facedown on the table. Then you ask someone from the audience to cut the deck. The two cards that he chooses have the same numbers and colors as the two cards you pulled out.

The Trick

1. Shuffle the deck. Tell your audience you're going to choose two cards that will be the same number and color that anyone from the audience will pick later.

2. Look through the cards. Pretend to be thinking hard. What you're really doing is looking at the top and bottom cards.

3. Pick out two cards that match the top and bottom cards' number and color. For example, if the top card is the Three of Clubs and the bottom card is the Six of Diamonds, you pick out the Three of Spades and the Six of Hearts.

4. Place your two cards facedown on the table.

5. Put the deck facedown on the table and ask someone from your audience to cut the deck into two piles. Pick up the bottom half and place it on top of the other half, but place it sideways across the deck so that the cards look like a plus sign.

6. Go over the trick so far with your audience. Tell them that you shuffled the deck and took out two cards. Then you had your friend cut the deck anywhere he wanted. By talking like this, you're making your audience forget which half of the deck was the original top half and which half was the original bottom half.

7. Pick up the top half of the deck. Turn it faceup and place it on the table. Then turn over the top card of the other half.

8. Turn over the two cards that you placed facedown on the table. They will match the numbers and colors of the two faceup cards on the deck.

Dealing the Aces

The Magic

You show four Aces and put them on top of the deck. You deal the top four cards to yourself and the next four to your audience. When all the cards are turned over, your audience has the Aces.

Before You Start

Take out the four Aces and four other cards. Put all the Aces facedown in one pile. Put the four other cards facedown on top of them. Pick up these cards and turn the pack faceup. You're ready to start.

4 Other Cards behind the 4 Aces.

The Trick

1. Spread out the four Aces so your audience can see them. Make sure you don't show the four other cards. They should be hiding behind the last Ace.

2. Square up the packet, turn it facedown. Place it on top of the deck.

3. Deal the first four cards (which are not the Aces) facedown to yourself. Deal the next four cards (which are the Aces) facedown to your audience. Your audience will believe that you have the four Aces.

4. Make a magical pass over all the cards. Turn them over and show that your audience has the four Aces.

Four other cards hidden behind

1.

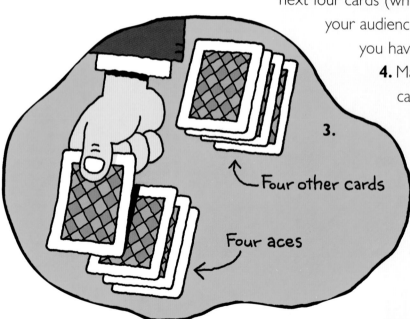

3.

Four other cards

Four aces

Royal Party

The Magic

You use some cards to tell a story about four royal families that had a big party. All the families were together, then they became mixed up in a storm. Magically, you show all the men, women, and children from each family together.

The Trick

1. Take out all the face cards (the Kings, Queens, Jacks) and all the Aces. Put away the rest of the deck.

2. Deal out the four Kings faceup. Tell your audience that four Kings were having a party.

3. Deal out the four Queens faceup. Place one Queen on top of each King. Make sure the suits match.

4. Tell your audience that the Kings invited their Queens.

5. Deal out the four Jacks faceup. Place one Jack on top of each Queen. Again, make sure that the suits match.

6. Tell your audience that the royal couples invited their sons.

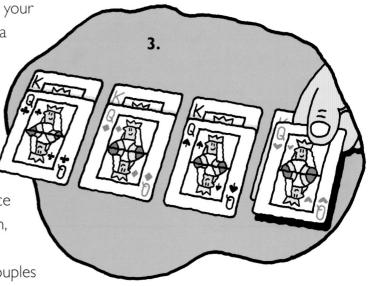

7. Tell your audience that a storm came, so everyone locked himself into his rooms.

8. Deal out the four Aces faceup. Place one Ace on top of each Jack. Make sure that the suits match.

9. Tell your audience to pretend that the Aces are the locks on the doors.

10. Square up each pile. Place one pile on top of the other pile until you make a small deck. Turn the deck facedown.

11. You can cut this packet as many times as you like. You can also ask someone in your audience to cut the packet. Make sure you don't shuffle the packet—only keep cutting it.

12. Tell your audience that the storm scared everyone. It shook the castle and rattled the locks on the doors.

13. Deal out four cards facedown. Deal them out from the top of the deck and have the cards go from left to right.

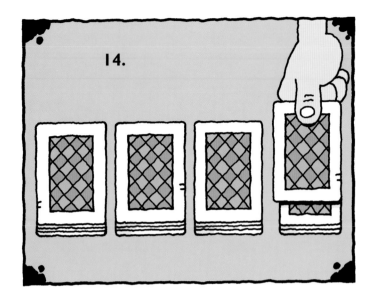

14. After you deal out the fourth card, deal out another four cards on top of these. Remember to deal from the left to the right. Keep dealing out the cards this way until you have four piles of cards.

15. Tell your audience that it was a magic storm. When it was over, all the Kings were together in one room, all the Queens in another, all the Jacks in another, and all the locks in another.

16. Turn each pile face up. There will be one pile of Kings, one of Queens, one of Jacks, and one of Aces.

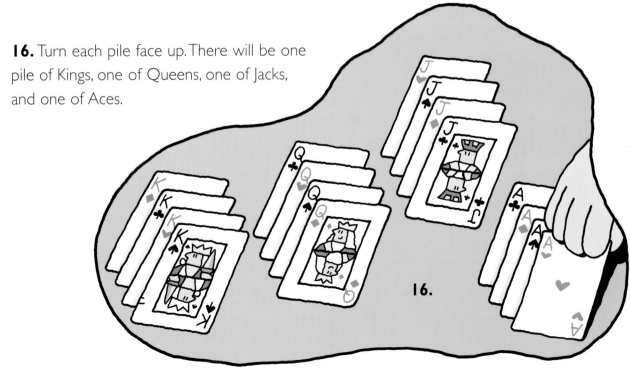

The Magic Starts Here

Welcome to the world of magic tricks! This section will show you many amazing tricks that you can easily do. But you'll need to make sure you have all your magic supplies before you start. Take this book and look through your house for the things that we have listed here. Ask an adult to help you if you can't find some of them.

- ✦ Some string
- ✦ A pair of safety scissors
- ✦ Clear tape
- ✦ Drinking glasses
- ✦ Ice cubes
- ✦ A salt shaker
- ✦ Salt and pepper

- ✦ Some small coins
- ✦ A napkin
- ✦ A comb
- ✦ A pencil and pen
- ✦ A ruler
- ✦ A small button
- ✦ A pop bottle

- ✦ A rubber band
- ✦ Paper money
- ✦ Black and red checker pieces
- ✦ Some balloons
- ✦ A pin

Like all good magicians, make sure you do each of these tricks many times before you show them to an audience. If a trick is too hard, ask an adult to help you. Then try out the tricks in front of a mirror or with a close friend who won't tell your magic secrets to anyone.

Once you can do the tricks smoothly, try to think of different ways to show them to people. You can make up a story to go along with the trick, or you can say that you have magical powers while you are doing the trick. But whatever way you choose, remember to have fun!

The Art of Knot Throwing

The Magic

Holding a piece of string in one hand, you make a knot magically appear.

Magic Supplies

✦ *A piece of string or rope*

Before You Start

Tie a big knot at one end of the string. Hold that end in your hand so that no one sees the knot.

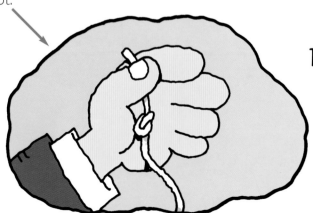

The Trick

1. Hold the end of the string with the knot in your left hand. Tell your audience you can make the string tie a knot all by itself.

2. With your right hand, bring the bottom end of the string up so both ends are in your left hand.

3. Pretend you're doing something very tricky. Then throw the end without the knot down. Do this two times.

4. On the third time, throw down the end of the string that has the knot in it. It will look as though you made the knot magically appear.

The Knot Challenge

The Magic

Ask your friend to tie a knot in a piece of string without letting go of the ends. She can't do it, but you can.

Magic Supplies

✦ *A long piece of string*   ✦ *A table*

The Trick

1. Hold one end of the string in each hand. Give it to your friend and ask her to tie a knot in the string without letting go of either end. After she tries a few times, take the string back and lay it out on the table.
2. Fold your arms and then pick up the string. Pick up one end at a time.
3. Without letting go of the ends of the string, unfold your arms. There will be a knot in the string!

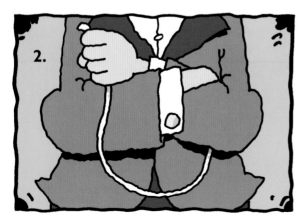
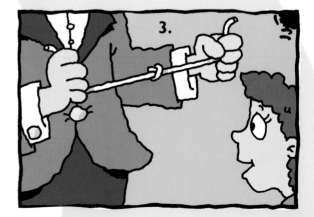

Cut & Restored String

The Magic

You cut a piece of string in two. Then, with a magic word, the string becomes one piece again.

Magic Supplies

✦ *Two pieces of string or yarn. One should be at least as long as your arm; the other piece should be about as long as your hand, like in the pictures below. Make sure that you can easily cut the string or yarn.*
✦ *A pair of safety scissors*　　✦ *Clear tape*

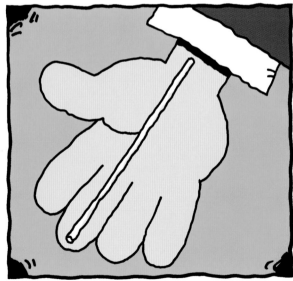

Before You Start

Take the small piece of string. Hold the ends together and use a small piece of tape to join them.

Keep this small loop of string with your scissors. Put them near you, but don't let your audience see them.

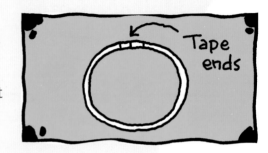

The Trick

1. Show the long piece of string to your audience. You can even let them hold it and check it.

2. Bring the two ends of the long string together and find the middle point. Fold it there and hold it in your left hand. Make a fist so that no one sees the fold. Your audience should only see the two ends of string hanging from the bottom of your left fist.

3. Pick up your scissors with your right hand and secretly pick up the small loop of string with your left hand. The easiest way to do this is to have the small loop of string and scissors in a box or a bag

behind you. That way, you have to turn away from the audience and no one will see what you're doing.

4. Make sure the bend of the small loop sticks out from the top of your left fist. Your audience will believe this is the bend in the long piece of string. Turn around to face your audience.

5. Carefully cut the loop in half (or get someone from your audience to do it). Then, keep cutting the ends that are sticking out from the top of your fist. Let the pieces fall to the floor.

6. Make sure to let all the pieces of the small piece of string fall to the floor. Cut through the tape, too. When you're done, you're holding only the bend of the long piece of string in your left fist.

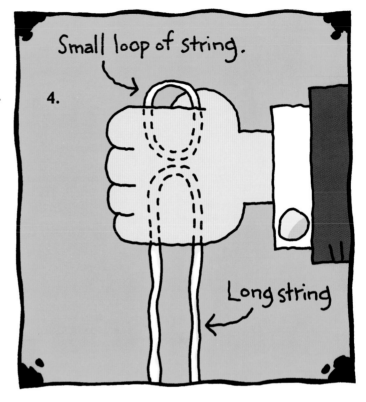

Small loop of string.

4.

Long string

5.

7. Put the scissors down. Bring all of the long string into your left hand. Say your magic word. Then open up your left hand and pull out the string to show that it is one piece again.

Melting String

The Magic

You put two pieces of string into your friend's hand. When you pull the strings out, they've melted into one piece.

Magic Supplies

✦ *A piece of string about half as long as your arm. You need to find the kind of string that's made from several smaller strands twisted together, such as a yo-yo string.*

Before You Start

Take hold of the string at its middle and untwist it by rolling it carefully between your thumb and first finger.

Once you can see separate strands of the string, pull some to the left and some to the right. As you pull them apart, twist these strands together so that they look like the rest of the string. Keep pulling until it looks like a "+" sign.

Hold the middle point of the string between the thumb and first finger in your left hand. Bring the ends of the strings that you had pulled apart above your thumb and first finger. Then bring the end of the middle string down.

When you hold it at the middle point, it looks as though you're holding two separate pieces of string. Now you're ready to start the trick.

  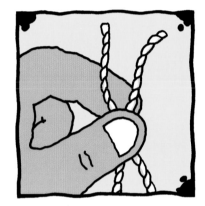

The Trick

1. Hold the string and tell your audience you're going to show them a trick with these "two pieces" of string. Ask someone from your audience to hold her palm out.

2. Put the short ends of the string into her palm. Then place one of the long ends over the thumb side of her hand. Place the other long end over the little-finger side of her hand.

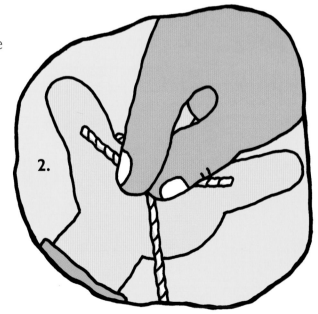

2.

3. Tell her to close her fingers around the string. Take your thumb and first finger from her palm right before her fingers close. Make sure the right-side and left-side ends don't stick out from her fist. Ask her to turn her fist so that her palm faces down.

4. Take one end of the string in each hand. Slowly pull the string back and forth a tiny bit.

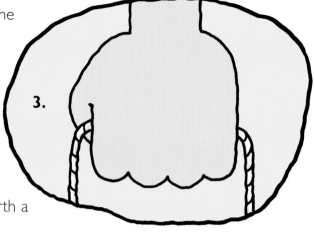

The short ends of the string will come apart and wind back into the rest of the string so that it will look like one piece of string again.

5. Keep pulling the string back and forth a few times. Then pull the string all the through her fist. It looks as if you just joined two pieces of string together.

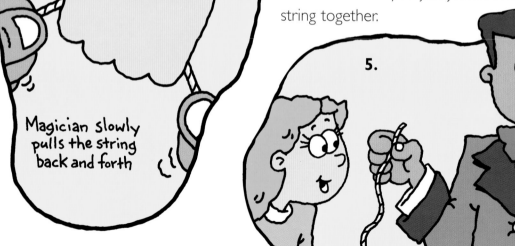

Magician slowly pulls the string back and forth

Sticky Ice

The Magic

You show a glass of water with an ice cube floating in it. You give your friend a short piece of string and ask him to use the string to lift the ice cube out of the glass. He can't do it, but you can.

Magic Supplies

◆ *A glass of water*
◆ *An ice cube*
◆ *A piece of string a few inches long*
◆ *Some salt*

The Trick

1. Give someone from your audience a glass of water with an ice cube floating in it. Then give him a piece of string and say that he can't use it to lift the ice cube out of the glass. As much as he tries, he won't be able to do it.

2. Now it's your turn. Lay the string across the top of the glass so that the middle of the string rests on top of the ice cube.

3. Sprinkle some salt on the ice cube. Wait for a while, then lift the string. The ice cube will be frozen to it.

The Disappearing Salt Shaker

The Magic

You place a coin on the table and tell your audience that you'll make the coin disappear. You cover the coin with a salt shaker and then cover that with a napkin. To everyone's surprise, you press down on the napkin. When you lift the napkin, the coin is still there, but the salt shaker has disappeared.

Magic Supplies

+ A small coin   + A salt shaker   + A napkin that's big enough to cover the salt shaker
+ A table covered with a tablecloth   + A chair

The Trick

1. Sit on the chair behind the table. Place the coin on the table in front of you. Tell your audience that you're going to make the coin disappear.

2. Spread the napkin on top of it and then pretend to change your mind. Tell them you're going to make the trick harder.

3. Lift the napkin and place the salt shaker on top of the coin.

4. Place the napkin over the shaker. Wrap your right hand around the napkin and shaker so that the napkin will have the shape of the shaker.

4.

5. Lift the shaker up and look at the coin. Ask your audience what kind of coin it is. Bring your right hand close to the edge of the table. Point at the coin with your left hand and move the coin around on the tabletop.

6. Secretly relax your right fingers a little bit and let the salt shaker fall into your lap. Keep holding the napkin as if the salt shaker were under it. The napkin will keep its shape.

7. Pretending that the shaker is still under the napkin, cover the coin with the napkin.

8. Ask the audience whether the coin was heads-up or tails-up. This will make them think about the coin and not about the salt shaker.

9. Surprise everyone by pressing the top of the napkin down onto the table. Open up the napkin and show that the shaker has vanished.

10. To make the salt shaker reappear, you can reach under the table and secretly pick up the shaker from your lap. Show your audience the shaker and tell them that it must have gone right through the table.

Combing Out the Pepper

The Magic

You mix a little bit of salt and pepper together into a small pile on the table. Then ask someone from your audience to separate the pepper from the salt without touching the pile with his fingers. He can't do it, but you can.

Magic Supplies

✦ *Salt and pepper* ✦ *A comb*

The Trick

1. Mix a small amount of salt and pepper on the table. Ask someone from your audience to separate the pepper from the salt without touching either.

2. After your friend gives up, it's your turn. Take a comb and run it through your hair a few times. This will give the comb a charge of electricity. Then drag the comb over the pile of salt and pepper.

3. The pepper grains will come to the electric charge. Because they're lighter than the grains of salt, they'll stick to the comb!

Wavy Pencil

The Magic

You're able to make any pencil appear to be made of rubber!

Magic Supply

✦ *A pencil (or pen)*

The Trick

1. Hold the end of the pencil between your thumb and first finger. Hold it sideways in front of your face.

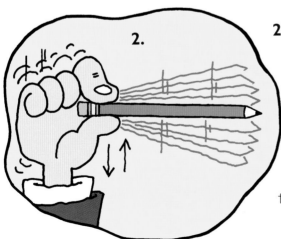

2. Move your hand straight up and down in a short, smooth way. Make sure you hold the pencil loosely. Don't wiggle it with your thumb and first finger. Move your whole hand. It should wobble a little bit as you move your hand.

You will need to practice moving your hand a few times before you find the right way to make the pencil seem to bounce like rubber.

The Magnetic Pen 1

The Magic

A pen magically sticks to your hand.

Magic Supply

✦ *A pen*

The Trick

1. Hold the pen in your left hand and close your fingers into a fist. The pen should stick out from both sides of your fist. Turn your body so that your audience is looking at the back of your left hand.
2. Hold your left wrist with your right hand. Tell your audience that you're doing this to keep your hand still.

2.

3. When you take hold of your left wrist, secretly straighten the first finger of your right hand, so it holds the pen under your left fist.

4. Straighten the fingers of your left hand. The pen will appear to be stuck to your palm.

The Magnetic Pen 2

Here's another way you can do the Magnetic Pen trick. This will fool people who think they know how you did the trick.

Magic Supplies

✦ A ruler
✦ A wristwatch or a shirt (or sweater) with tight cuffs on the wrist

Before You Start

Hide the ruler in your left sleeve. The ruler should be along the inside of your wrist. The end of it should be very close to the bottom part of your palm. If you're wearing a watch, you can tuck the end of the ruler under your watchstrap.

The Trick

1. Do the Magnetic Pen #1 (see pages 68–69).

2. Close your left hand around the pen and tell your audience you'll do the trick again. While you're talking, secretly pull the ruler out from under your sleeve. Pull out enough of it to hold the pen in place.

3. Perform the trick as you did for Magnetic Pen #1. Then let go of your left wrist and show that your right hand is nowhere near the pen.

4. When you're done, take hold of your left wrist again and secretly tuck the ruler back up your sleeve.

The Magnetic Pen 3

And here's the last way to do the Magnetic Pen trick.

The Trick

1. Place the pen on your left palm and hold it down with your left thumb.

2. Bring your hands together. Interlace your fingers, but secretly keep your right middle finger inside your palm.

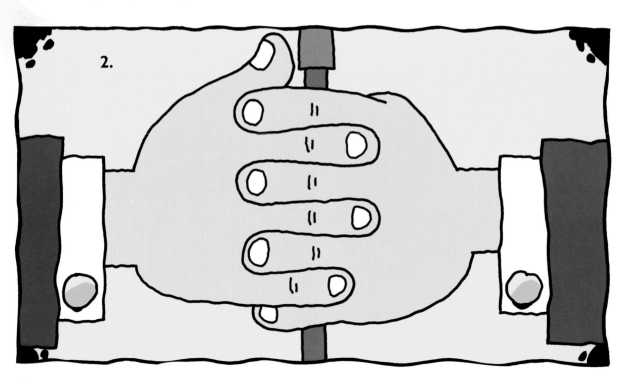

3. Raise your hands so that your audience is looking at the backs of your hands.

4. Use your thumbs to push the pen between the back of your right middle finger and your left palm. Say a few magic words and then tell everyone that you have turned the pen into a magnet.

5. Let go with one thumb and then another. The pen will look as though it is stuck to your hands.

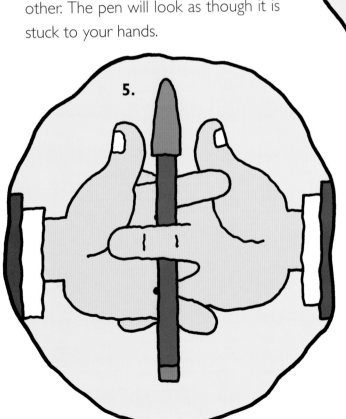

6. Open up your hands and let the pen fall. That way, no one will notice that your right middle finger was hidden.

The Disappearing Pen

The Magic

You hold a small coin and tell your audience that when you tap it with your pen, the coin will disappear. When you tap the coin, the pen disappears!

You show the audience where the pen went. When they look back at your hand, the coin has now disappeared.

Magic Supplies

✦ A small coin   ✦ A pen
✦ A jacket with an open left side pocket or pants with large pockets

The Trick

1. Show the coin on the palm of your left hand. Your audience should be on your left side. Hold the pen in your right hand.
2. Tell your audience that you'll make the coin disappear by tapping it with the pen. Raise the pen up so that it's by your right ear. Then bring your arm down and tap the coin. Do this again.

2.

3. Raise your pen for the third time. But before you tap the coin, slide the pen behind your right ear. Then bring your hand down as if you're still holding the pen and you're ready to tap the coin.

4. Before you tap the coin, pretend that you're surprised to see that the pen has disappeared. Show your audience that your right hand is empty.

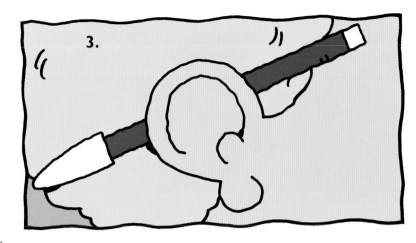

5. Pretend to look for the pen. Turn the right side of your body to your audience so that they will see the pen behind your ear. When they tell you it's there, remove it with your right hand.

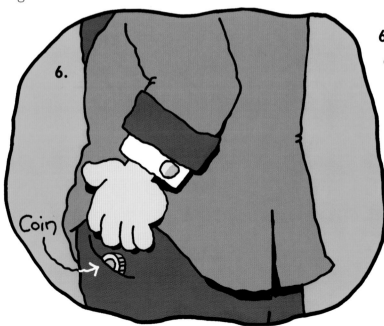

6. While you're doing this, secretly drop the coin into your left side pocket. Hold your left hand as if you're still holding the coin.

7. Turn back to your audience and pretend to tap the coin as you did before. Open your palm and show that the coin has disappeared.

The Rubber Spoon

The Magic

You seem to bend the handle of a spoon nearly in half and then quickly straighten it again.

Magic Supply

✦ A spoon ✦ A table

The Trick

1. Hold the spoon in your left hand like in the picture below:

2. Bring your hands together. Place your right fingers in front of your left fingers. Secretly move your left little finger so that you're holding the handle of the spoon between it and your third left finger. It should look as if you're holding the handle of the spoon with both hands.

3. Press the bowl of the spoon on the table and slowly tilt your hands forward as if you're bending the handle of the spoon forward.

4. Secretly let the handle of the spoon slide between your hands. It will look as though you're bending the spoon.

5. To magically straighten it, lift your hands. Take hold of the bowl of the spoon with your right hand. Your left hand should look as if you're really holding a bent spoon. With your right hand, slowly pull the spoon from your left hand. Your spoon is magically straight again!

Floating Button

The Magic

You drop a small shirt button into a glass filled with some soft drink. The button sinks to the bottom. At your command, the button floats to the top of the glass. When you tell it to sink, the button falls back to the bottom of the glass.

Magic Supplies

✦ *A small and light button*   ✦ *A glass full of clear soft-drink*

Before You Start

You will need to find out how long it takes for your button to rise and sink in the soft drink. Count in your head how long it takes and remember these times when you do the trick.

The Trick

1. Drop the button into a glass full of clear soft drink. The button will sink to the bottom. Bubbles from the drink will stick to the button.

2. Count in your head how long it will take for enough bubbles to stick to the button and make it float to the top. Right before the button begins to float up, pretend to tell the button to rise.

3. After the button floats to the top of the soft drink, the bubbles on it will burst and the button will sink back to the bottom of the glass. Again, you will know how long this takes. Right before the button begins to sink down, pretend to tell the button to go down. The button will keep going up and down as long as there are bubbles in your drink.

A Drink of Water

The Magic

You hold a glass of water in your right hand and have your friend hold your right wrist. No matter how hard he holds your wrist in place, you can lift the glass to your lips and have a drink.

Magic Supply

✦ *A glass of water*

The Trick

1. Hold the glass of water in your right hand and ask someone from your audience to hold your right wrist. Tell him that no matter how hard he holds your right arm in place, you'll be able to lift the glass to your lips and have a drink. Make sure that he doesn't hold your wrist so hard that he's hurting you or that he makes you spill the water. Tell him just to hold your arm in place.

2. Ask him when he's ready. When he says, "OK," use your left hand to take the glass and drink from it!

Ghost in the Bottle

The Magic

You place a small coin over the opening of a bottle and tell your audience that you've just trapped a ghost inside the bottle. After a few moments, the coin starts to jump as if a spirit is trying to push it up from inside the bottle.

Magic Supplies

+ *An empty glass soft-drink bottle*
+ *A small, light coin that just fits over the bottle's opening*

Before You Start

Place the empty bottle in your freezer overnight. Take it out just before you're ready to do this trick.

The Trick

1. Once the bottle is out of the freezer, some water will begin to appear on the sides of the bottle. Secretly wipe off some water onto your finger.

2. Secretly wipe the drops of water around the edge of the coin. Then put the coin over the top of the bottle. The water should seal the opening between the coin and the top of the bottle.

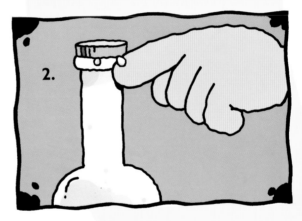

3. Tell your audience about the ghost that you've just trapped. Hold the bottle tightly with both hands. This will warm up the air inside the bottle. The air will try to escape around the edge of the coin.

4. After 15 to 20 seconds, the coin will start to move a little up and down. Let it do this for a while and then take your hands off the bottle. The coin should go on jumping for a few more seconds.

Coin Starts to Dance

The Hip-hopping Rubber Band

The Magic

You put a rubber band around your first two fingers and it magically jumps over to your last two fingers.

Magic Supply

✦ *A small rubber band*

The Trick

1. Put the rubber band around the first and second fingers of your left hand. Pull the rubber band down to the bottom of your fingers. Raise your hand so your palm faces you and your fingers are straight.

2. Close your left hand. With your right hand, take hold of the rubber band and wrap it around your left fingers like in Picture 2c.

   The audience is only seeing the back of your hand. To them it looks like the rubber band is around the bottom of your first two fingers.

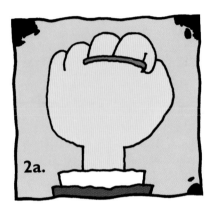

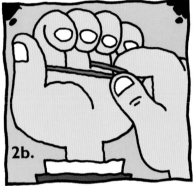

3. Say your magic word and open up your left hand. When you straighten your fingers, the rubber band will jump over to your third and little fingers.

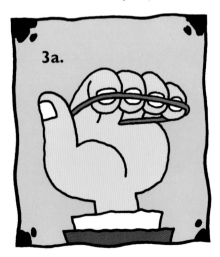

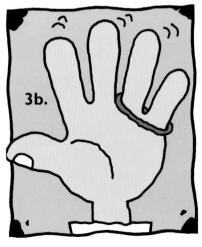

4. To make the rubber band jump back to the first two fingers, close your left hand into a fist. Wrap the rubber band around all four fingertips of your left hand. Straighten your fingers and the rubber band will jump again.

Upside-down Money

The Magic

You hold a bill right-side up in both hands. Slowly, you fold the bill. You never turn it over. When you unfold it, the bill has magically turned upside down.

Magic Supply

✦ *Any bill*

The Trick

1. Hold the bill with both hands. Fold the top half forward and down.

2. Fold the right half to the left.

3. Fold the right half to the left again.

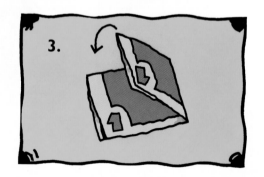

4. To open the bill so that it is right-side up again, unfold the back half of the bill to the right.

5. Unfold the front half of the bill to the left.

6. Now lift the front half of the bill. It's still right-side up. No magic has happened yet.

7. To make the bill magically unfold upside down, first do steps 1–3 to fold up the bill.

8. To open the bill so that it is up-side down, unfold the back half of the bill to the right. (The same as step 4.)

9.

9. Open the back half of the bill to the left.

10. Now lift the front half of the bill. It is now upside down.

10.

Coin Energy

The Magic

You place three coins on the table. Two coins are touching (let's call them coins A and B). The third (let's call it coin C) is a little bit apart from them.

Ask someone from your audience to put coin C between coins A and B, but he cannot move coin B and he cannot touch coin A. He can't do it, but you can.

Magic Supplies

✦ *Three small coins*   ✦ *A table*

The Trick

1. Lay the coins A, B, and C on the table. Have coins A and B touching. Coin C is not touching them.

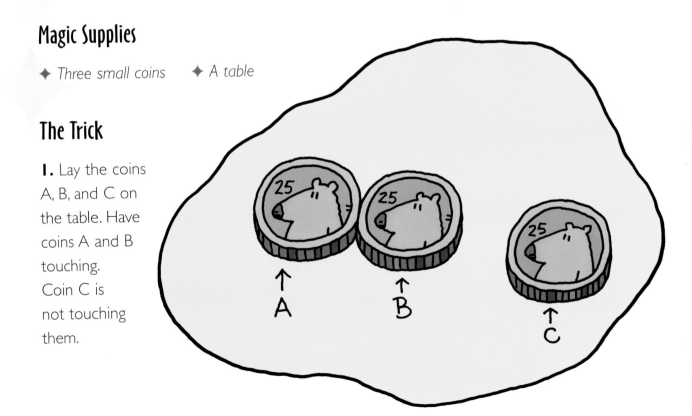

2. Ask someone from your audience to put coin C between coins A and B. Tell him that he has to do this without moving coin B and without touching coin A. After awhile, he will give up. Now it's your turn.

3. Place your first finger on coin B to keep it in place. With your other hand, slide coin C across the table so that it hits coin B. When coin C hits coin B, coin A will be knocked away.

4. Now you just have to move coin C to a place somewhere between coin A and coin B.

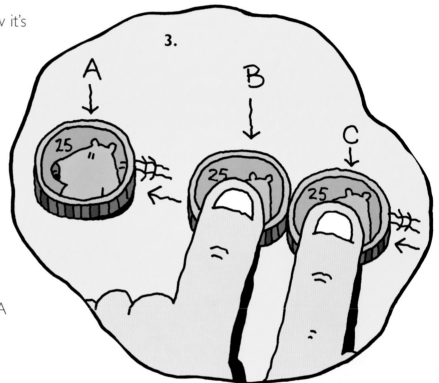

Checker Zapper

The Magic

You build a stack of black checker pieces with one red checker near the bottom. You ask your friend to take the red checker out without touching it or the rest of the stack. Magically, you're able to do it.

Magic Supplies

+ *Several black checker pieces and one red checker*
+ *A table*

The Trick

1. Stack the checker pieces. Make sure the red checker is the second piece from the bottom. Leave a few checker pieces lying on the table.

2. Ask someone from your audience if she can take the red checker out without touching it or the rest of the stack. When she gives up, you pick up one of the checker pieces that is lying on the table.

1.

3. Stand the checker piece on its edge so that it is not far from the stack. Aim it at the stack.

4. Press your first finger down on the edge of the checker so that it shoots into the stack of checkers. It should only knock out the red checker. Before you do this trick in front of an audience, you will need to practice it a few times to find the best place for putting the red checker. Sometimes it may be better to put the red checker third from the bottom.

Red Knocked out

Un-pop-able Balloon

The Magic

You're able to make some balloons stick to the wall. Then you're able to stick a pin into one of them without popping it. When you relax your magical powers, the balloon pops.

Magic Supplies

+ *A few balloons*   + *A pin*
+ *A roll of clear tape*

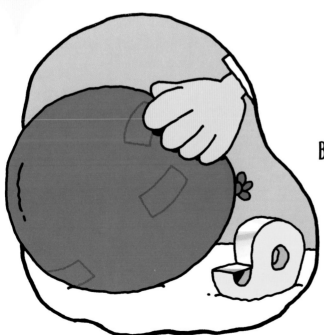

Before You Start

Blow up the balloons and tie them off. Stick a few pieces of clear tape on one of the balloons. Make sure to smooth down the edges of the tape so that no one can see them.

The Trick

1. Tell your audience that you have special magic powers over balloons. First, you will make them stick to the wall.

2. Rub any of the balloons **except** the one with the clear tape against your hair for a few moments. Then press them against the wall. They will stick.

3. Then tell your audience that you can make a balloon into a super-balloon. This super-balloon will not break if you stick it with a pin.

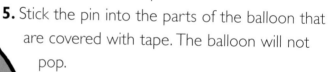

4. Pick up the balloon that has tape on it and pick up the pin. Make sure to be careful with the pin.

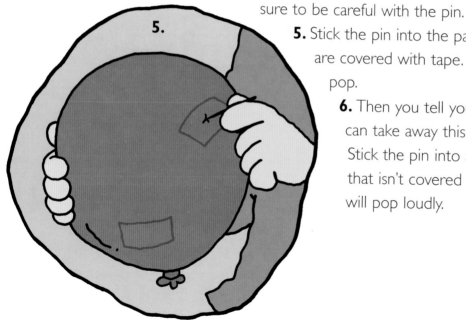

5. Stick the pin into the parts of the balloon that are covered with tape. The balloon will not pop.

6. Then you tell your audience that you can take away this balloon's super powers. Stick the pin into a part of the balloon that isn't covered with tape. Be ready, it will pop loudly.

Index